CLASSIC PIANO REPERTOIRE
EDNA MAE BURNAM

13 MEMORABLE PIANO SOLOS

ISBN 978-1-4768-7439-5

WILLIS MUSIC

EXCLUSIVELY DISTRIBUTED BY

HAL•LEONARD®
CORPORATION
7777 W. BLUEMOUND RD. P.O. BOX 13819 MILWAUKEE, WI 53213

Visit Hal Leonard Online at
www.halleonard.com

"**EDNA MAE BURNAM** was a pioneer in the piano pedagogy publishing field. I was privileged to work with her for many years, and she was an absolute delight. Every time we talked I left the conversation feeling upbeat and happy, and she had that effect on everyone she met. Edna Mae had the most wonderful outlook on life and delighted in helping people learn to make music. Today she is remembered as much for her whimsically titled pieces as she is for the effectiveness of those same pieces in piano studios around the world."

— Kevin Cranley, president and CEO of Willis Music
September 2012

EDNA MAE BURNAM (1907-2007) is best known as the author of the best-selling *A Dozen A Day* books. The technique series with the iconic stick-figure drawings that Burnam drew herself has sold over 30 million copies worldwide. Burnam was born in Sacramento, California and began piano lessons at age 7 with her mother, Armilda Mae Will. She would go on to major in piano at the University of Washington and Chico State College (now California State University at Chico), and ran a successful independent studio for decades. Her long and productive association with Willis Music began when she signed her first royalty contract in 1937. She followed up the success of *A Dozen A Day* with the *Step by Step* piano course, and in her lifetime composed hundreds of imaginative songs and pieces, including several based on observations she made in her travels abroad.

FROM THE PUBLISHERS

The *Classic Piano Repertoire* series includes popular as well as lesser-known pieces from a select group of composers out of the Willis piano archives (established in 1899). This volume features 13 wonderful piano solos by Edna Mae Burnam, progressing from early intermediate to early advanced. Each piece has been newly engraved and edited with the aim to preserve Burnam's original intent and musical purpose.

CONTENTS

4   Tempo Tarantelle *(1958)*

6   Longing for Scotland *(1980)*

8   Hawaiian Leis *(1961)*

10   Butterfly Time *(1955)*

12   Song of the Prairie *(1958)*

13   The White Cliffs of Dover *(1966)*

16   Lovely Señorita *(1962)*

20   Storm in the Night *(1973)*

24   Jubilee! *(1986)*

28   The Mighty Amazon River *(1989)*

31   Rumbling Rumba *(1985)*

36   Echoes of Gypsies *(1972)*

40   The Singing Fountain *(1954)*

Tempo Tarantelle

Edna Mae Burnam

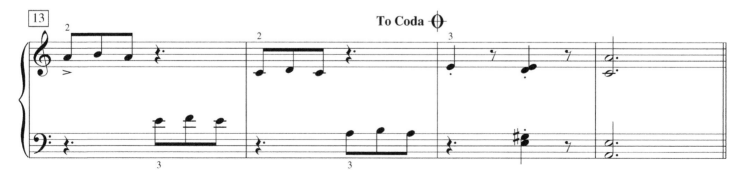

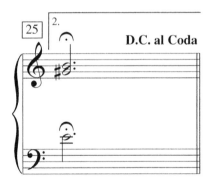

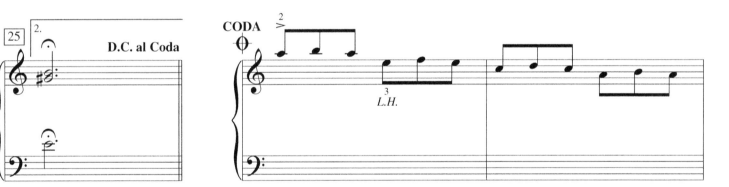

In memory of dear Annie Sutherland

Longing for Scotland

Edna Mae Burnam

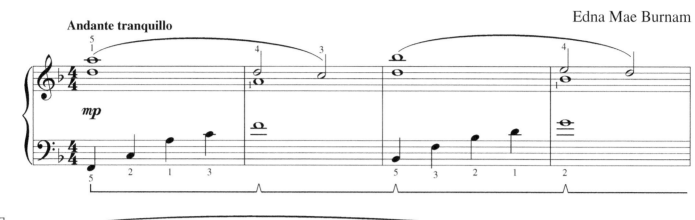

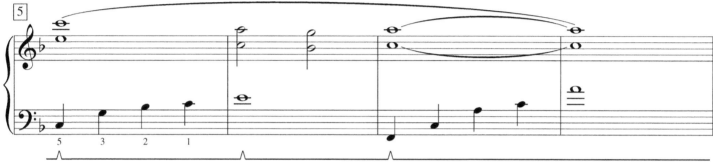

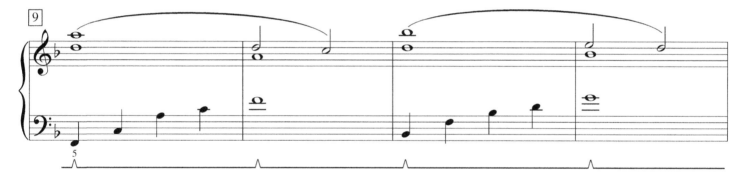

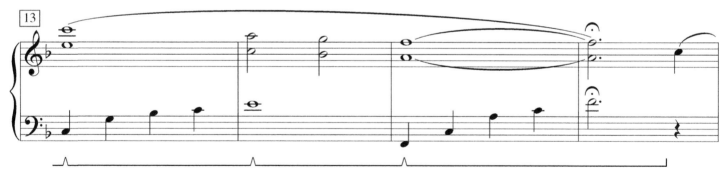

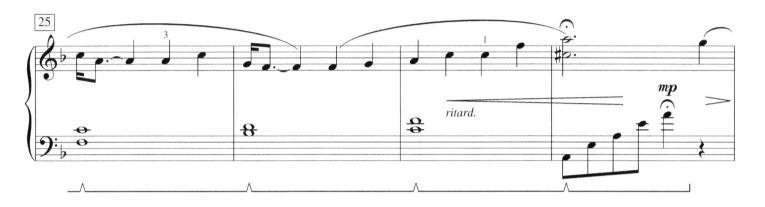

Tranquillo

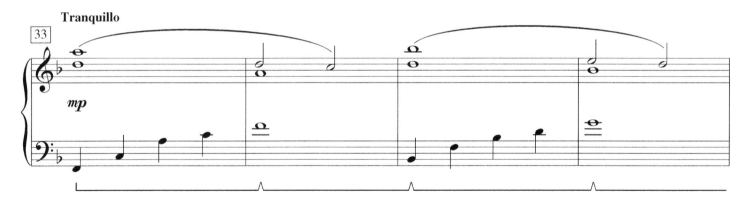

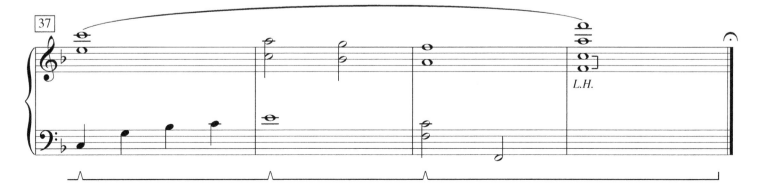

Hawaiian Leis

Edna Mae Burnam

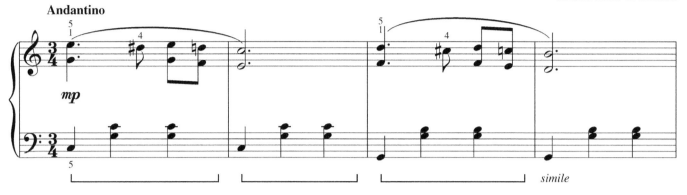

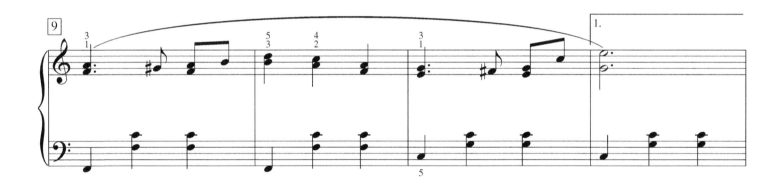

Butterfly Time

Edna Mae Burnam

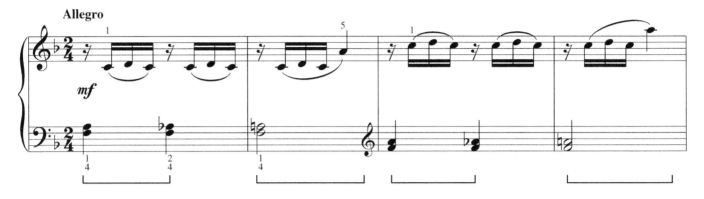

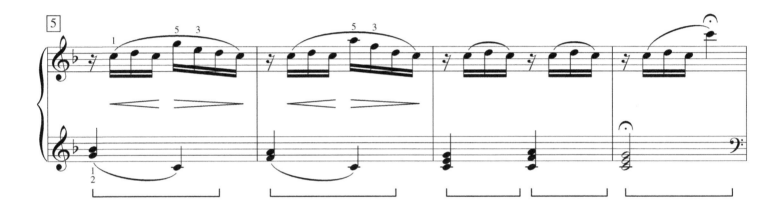

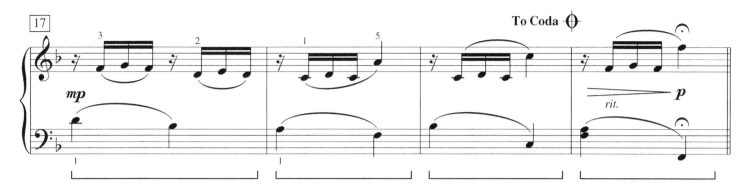

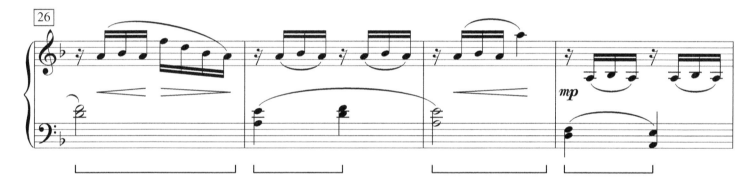

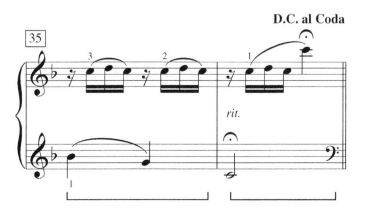

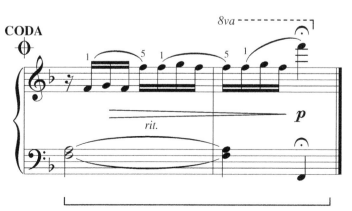

Song of the Prairie

Edna Mae Burnam

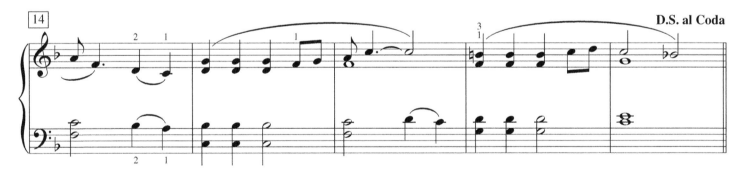

To Berenice Benson Bentley

The White Cliffs of Dover

Edna Mae Burnam

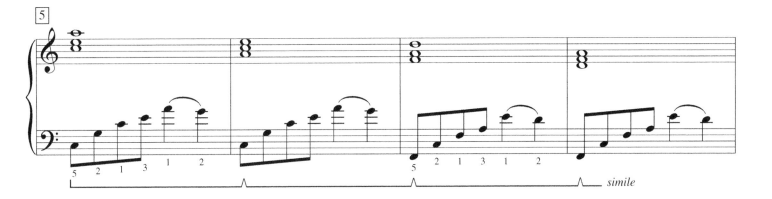

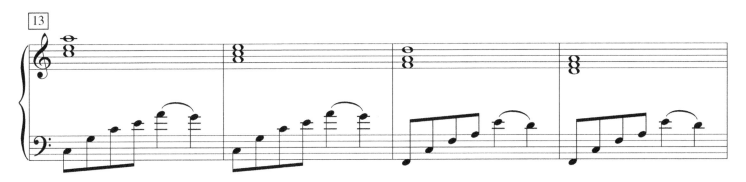

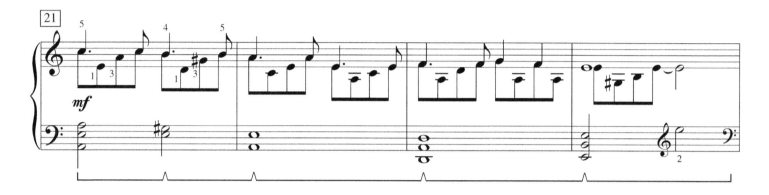

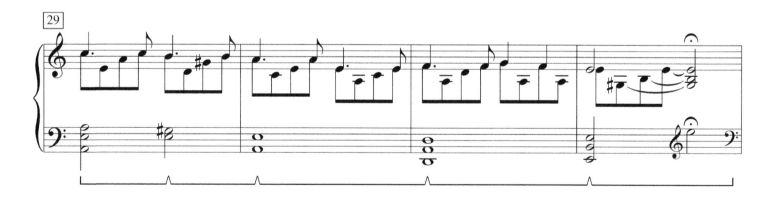

To Zue Geery Pease,
who was my piano teacher for many years.

Lovely Señorita

Edna Mae Burnam

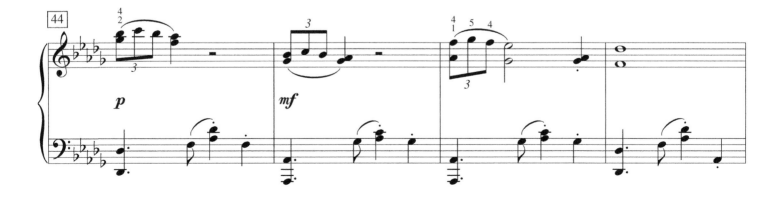

To Susan Kuske

Storm in the Night

Edna Mae Burnam

Moderato

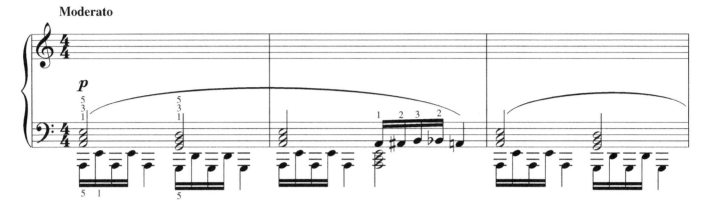

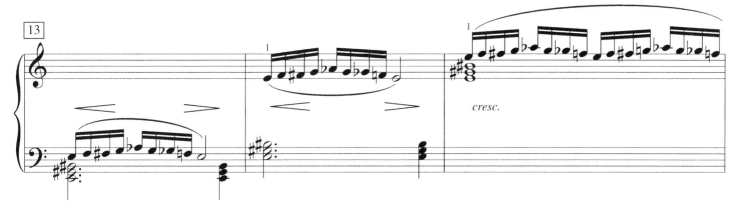

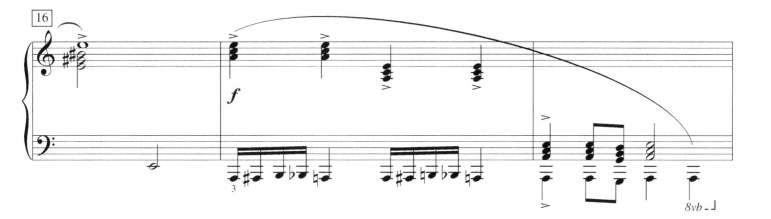

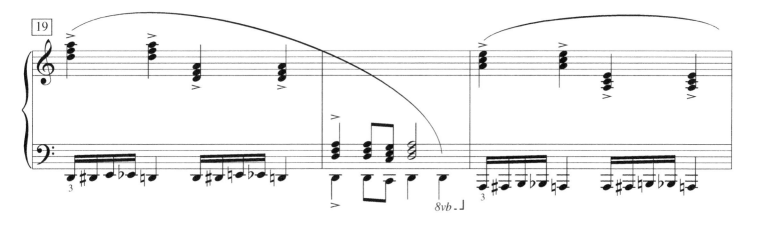

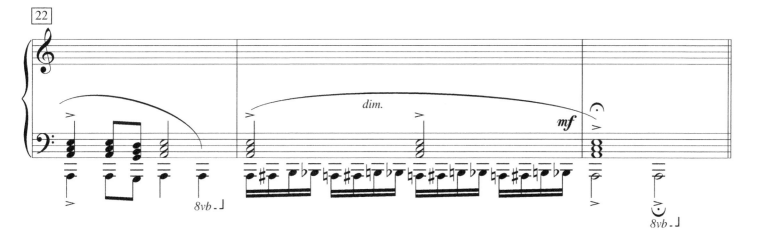

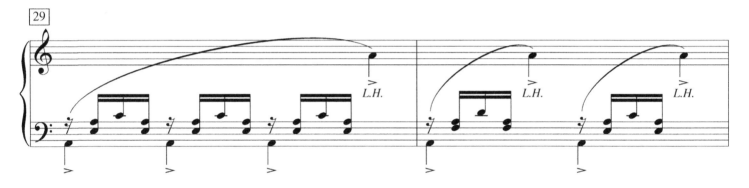

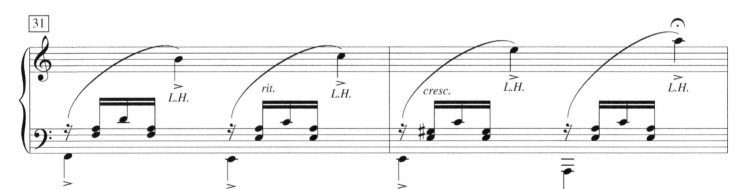

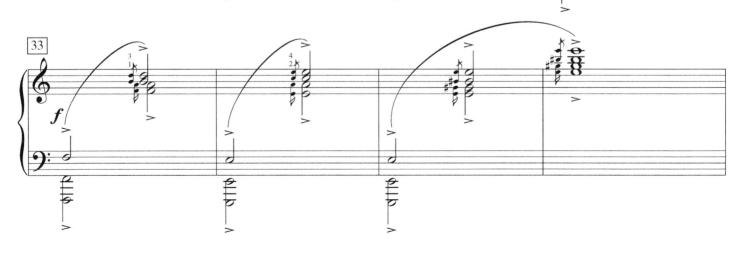

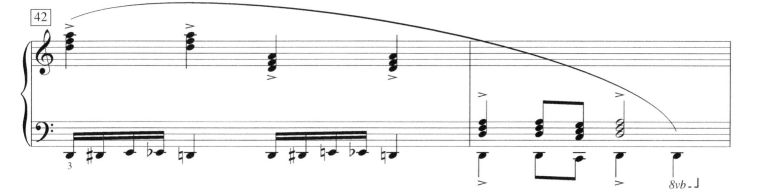

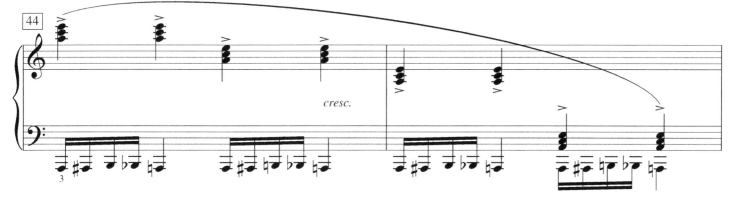

To Ruth Davis

Jubilee!

Edna Mae Burnam

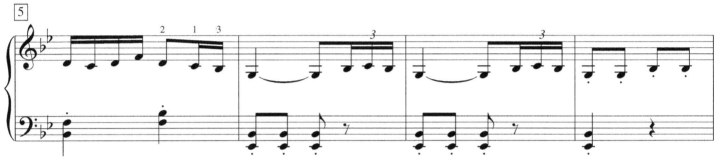

26

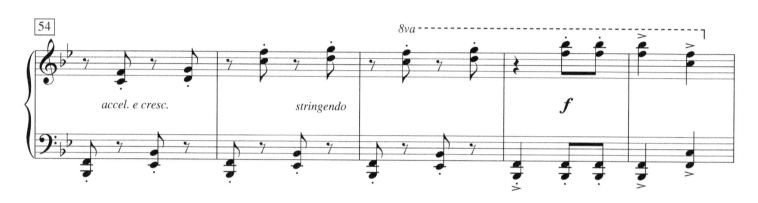

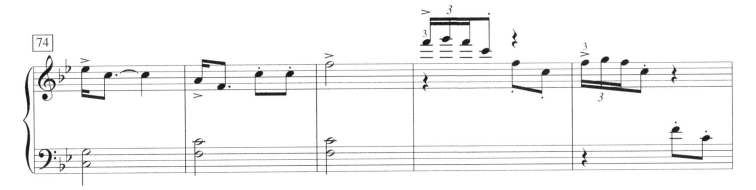

To my dear friend, Alleen Farrar

The Mighty Amazon River

Edna Mae Burnam

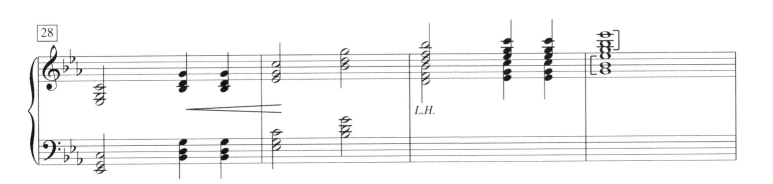

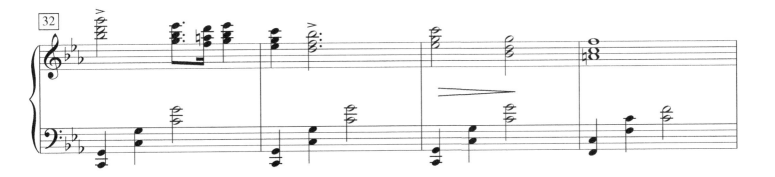

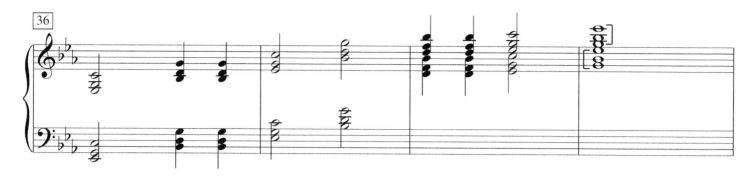

To my dear friend, Edna Smith Sibole

Rumbling Rumba

Edna Mae Burnam

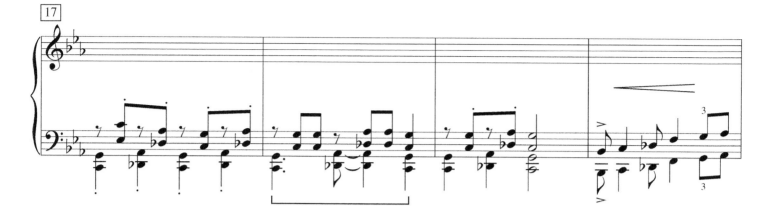

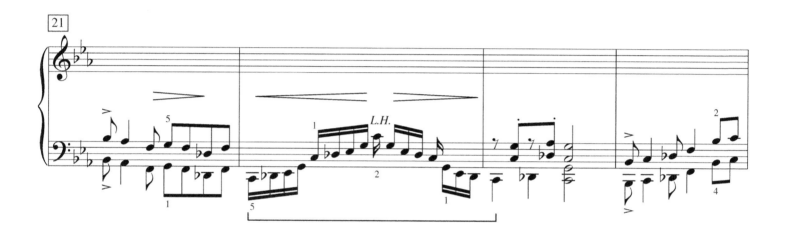

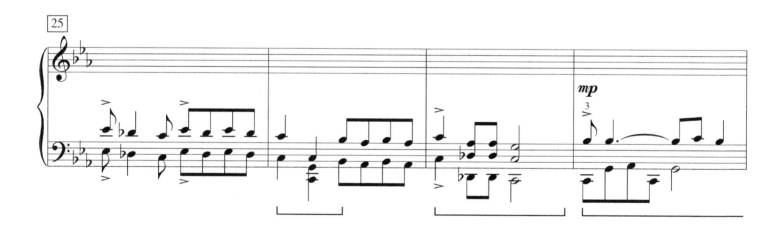

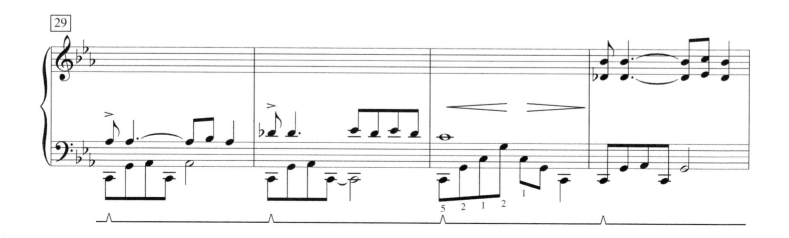

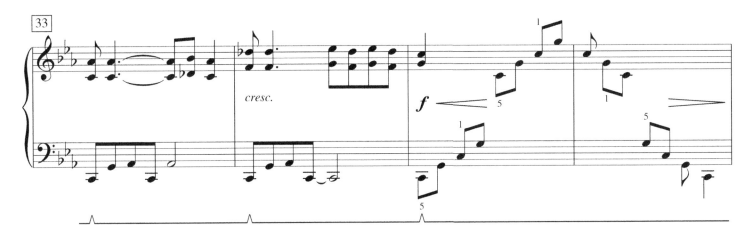

To my daughters — Peggy and Patricia

Echoes of Gypsies
(A Gypsy Fantasy)

Edna Mae Burnam

A la fantasy – moderato

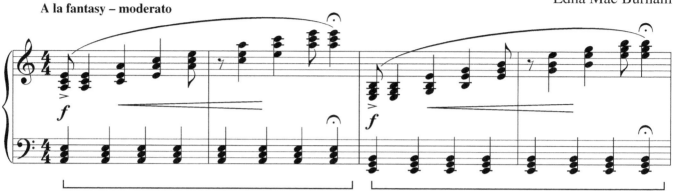

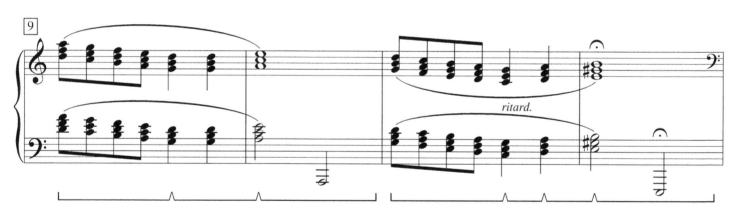

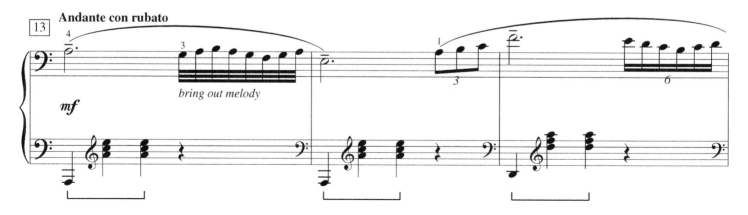

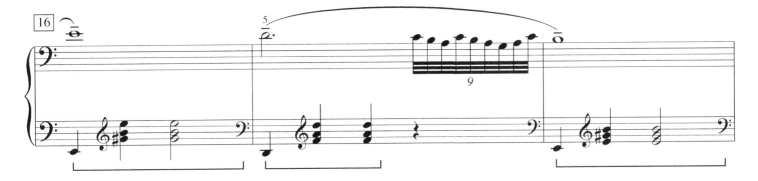

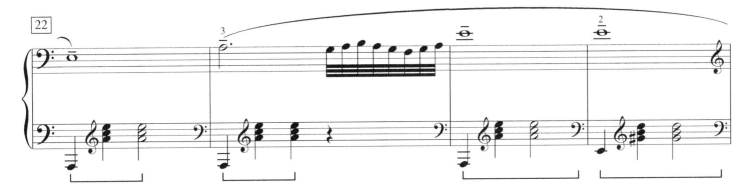

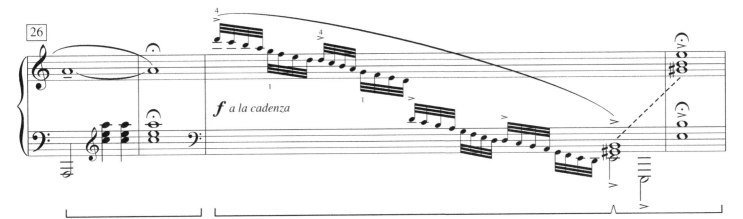

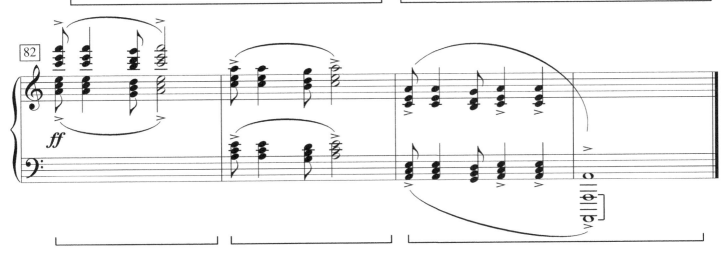

To Janice Booth

The Singing Fountain

Edna Mae Burnam

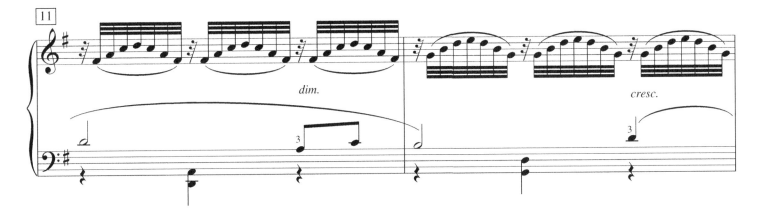

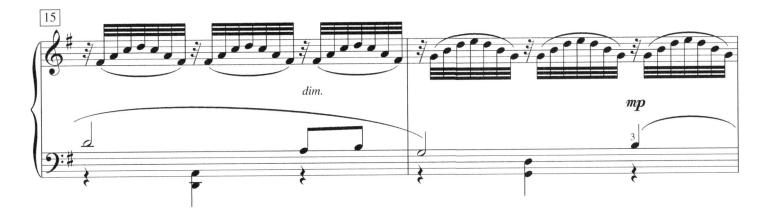

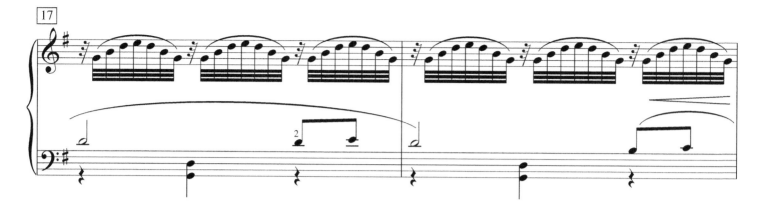

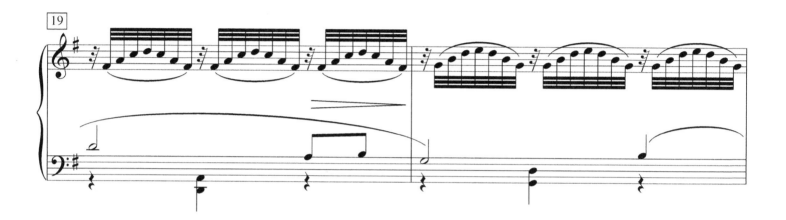

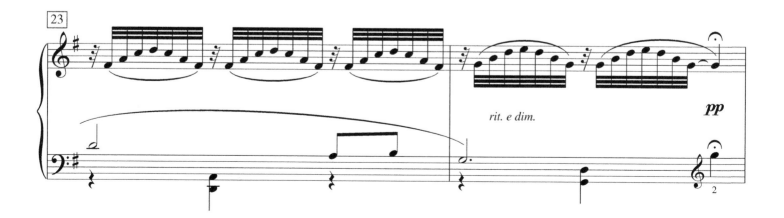

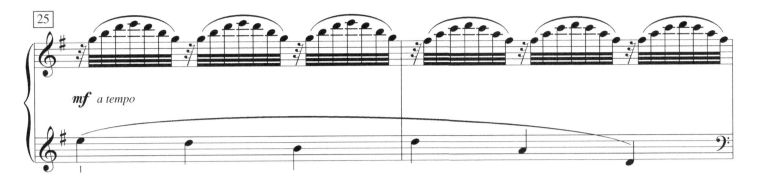

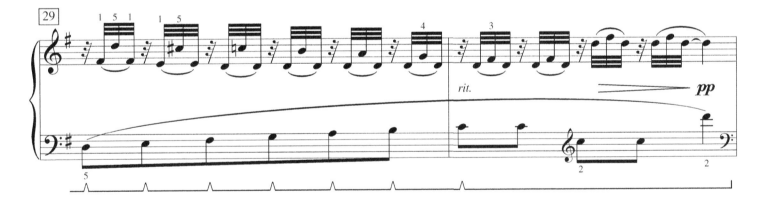

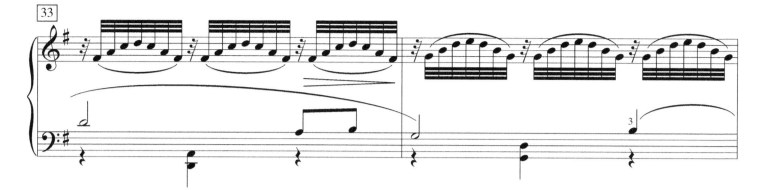

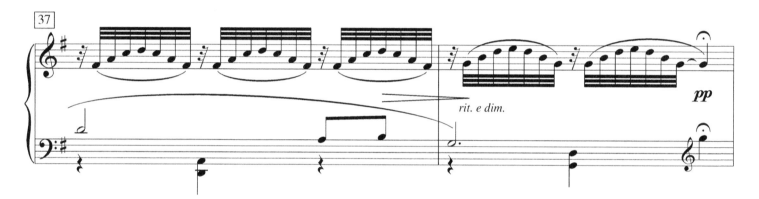

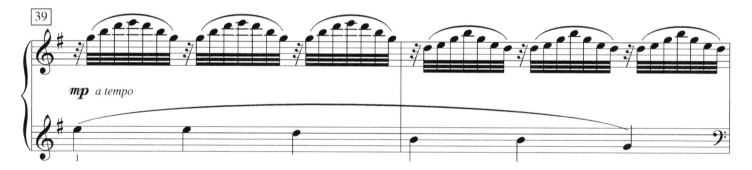

Spectacular Piano Solos

from

www.willispianomusic.com

Early Elementary

00416850 ____	Barnyard Strut/*Glenda Austin*	$2.99
00416702 ____	Big Green Frog/*Carolyn C. Setliff*	$2.99
00416904 ____	The Blizzard/*Glenda Austin*	$2.99
00416882 ____	Bow-Wow Blues/*Glenda Austin*	$2.99
00416883 ____	Catch Me!/*Frank Levin*	$2.99
00406670 ____	Cookies/*Carolyn Miller*	$2.95
00404218 ____	Fog at Sea/*William Gillock*	$2.95
00416907 ____	Guardian Angels/*Naoko Ikeda*	$2.99
00416918 ____	Halloween Surprise/*Ronald Bennett*	$2.99
00412099 ____	Moccasin Dance/*John Thompson*	$1.95
00416783 ____	My Missing Teeth/*Carolyn C. Setliff*	$2.95
00416933 ____	The Perceptive Detective/*Carolyn Miller*	$2.99
00416816 ____	Rain, Rain/*Carolyn Miller*	$2.99

Mid-Elementary

00416780 ____	The Acrobat/*Carolyn Miller*	$2.99
00416041 ____	Autumn Is Here/*William Gillock*	$2.99
00416902 ____	Cherokee Prayer of Peace/*Glenda Austin*	$2.99
00416803 ____	The Dancing Bears/*Carolyn Miller*	$2.99
00416878 ____	Mini Toccata/*Eric Baumgartner*	$2.99
00416958 ____	Miss Kitty Kat/*Glenda Austin*	$2.99
00404738 ____	Moonlight/*William Gillock*	$2.95
00416872 ____	The Rainbow/*Carolyn Miller*	$2.99
00416728 ____	Seahorse Serenade/*Carolyn C. Setliff*	$2.95
00416674 ____	Seaside Dancer/*Ronald Bennett*	$2.50
00416785 ____	Watermelon Sunset/*Randall Hartsell*	$2.95

Later Elementary

00416840 ____	At the Ballet/*Carolyn C. Setliff*	$2.99
00416852 ____	Black Cat Chat/*Eric Baumgartner*	$2.99
00416887 ____	Chromatic Craze/*Carolyn C. Setliff*	$2.99
00416786 ____	Egyptian Journey/*Randall Hartsell*	$2.95
00416906 ____	Evening Melody/*Naoko Ikeda*	$2.99
00416886 ____	Flying Fingers/*Carolyn C. Setliff*	$2.99
00416836 ____	The Gentle Brook/*Carolyn Miller*	$2.99
00416908 ____	The Goblins Gather/*Frank Levin*	$2.99
00405918 ____	Monkey on a Stick/*Lynn Freeman Olson*	$2.95
00416866 ____	October Leaves/*Carolyn C. Setliff*	$2.99
00406552 ____	Parisian Waltz/*Robert Donahue*	$2.95
00416781 ____	The Race Car/*Carolyn Miller*	$2.95
00416885 ____	Scaling the Peaks/*Randall Hartsell*	$2.99
00406564 ____	Showdown/*Ronald Bennett*	$2.95
00416919 ____	Sparkling Waterfall/*Carolyn C. Setliff*	$2.99
00416820 ____	Star Wonders/*Randall Hartsell*	$2.99
00416779 ____	Sunrise at San Miguel/*Ronald Bennett*	$2.99
00416828 ____	Tick Tock/*Eric Baumgartner*	$2.99
00416881 ____	Twilight Tarantella/*Glenda Austin*	$2.99

Early Intermediate

00416943 ____	Autumn Nocturne/*Susan Alcon*	$2.99
00405455 ____	Bass Train Boogie/*Stephen Adoff*	$2.99
00416817 ____	Broken Arm Blues/*Carolyn Miller*	$2.99
00416841 ____	The Bubbling Brook/*Carolyn Miller*	$2.99
00416849 ____	Bye-Bye Blues/*Glenda Austin*	$2.99
00416945 ____	Cafe Francais/*Jonathan Maiocco*	$2.99
00416834 ____	Canopy of Stars/*Randall Hartsell*	$2.99
00416956 ____	Dancing in a Dream/*William Gillock*	$2.99
00415585 ____	Flamenco/*William Gillock*	$2.95
00416856 ____	Garden of Dreams/*Naoko Ikeda*	$2.99
00416818 ____	Majestic Splendor/*Carolyn C. Setliff*	$2.99
00416948 ____	Manhattan Swing/*Naoko Ikeda*	$2.99

00416733 ____	The Matador/*Carolyn Miller*	$2.99
00416940 ____	Medieval Rondo/*Carolyn C. Setliff*	$2.99
00416942 ____	A Melancholy Night/*Naoko Ikeda*	$2.99
00416877 ____	Mystic Quest/*Randall Hartsell*	$2.99
00416873 ____	Le Papillon (The Butterfly)/*Glenda Austin*	$2.99
00416829 ____	Scherzo Nuovo/*Eric Baumgartner*	$2.99
00416947 ____	Snowflakes in Spring/*Naoko Ikeda*	$2.99
00416937 ____	Stampede/*Carolyn Miller*	$2.99
00416917 ____	Supernova/*Ronald Bennett*	$2.99
00416842 ____	Tarantella in G Minor/*Glenda Austin*	$2.99
00416782 ____	Toccata Caprice/*Carolyn C. Setliff*	$2.95
00416938 ____	Toccatina Tag/*Ronald Bennett*	$2.99
00416869 ____	Twilight Tapestry/*Randall Hartsell*	$2.99
00416924 ____	A Waltz to Remember/*Glenda Austin*	$2.99

Mid-Intermediate

00416848 ____	American Syncopations/*Eric Baumgartner*	$3.99
00416698 ____	Black Key Blues/*Alexander Peskanov*	$2.95
00416911 ____	Blues Streak/*Eric Baumgartner*	$2.99
00416855 ____	Dance of the Unicorn/*Naoko Ikeda*	$2.99
00416893 ____	Fantasia in A Minor/*Randall Hartsell*	$2.99
00416821 ____	Foggy Blues/*Naoko Ikeda*	$2.99
00414908 ____	Fountain in the Rain/*William Gillock*	$2.99
00416765 ____	Grand Sonatina in G/*Glenda Austin*	$2.95
00416875 ____	Himalayan Grandeur/*Randall Hartsell*	$2.99
00406630 ____	Jazz Suite No. 2/*Glenda Austin*	$3.95
00416910 ____	Little Rock (& Roll)/*Eric Baumgartner*	$2.99
00416939 ____	Midnight Fantasy/*Carolyn C. Setliff*	$2.99
00416857 ____	Moonlight Rose/*Naoko Ikeda*	$2.99
00414627 ____	Portrait of Paris/*William Gillock*	$2.99
00405171 ____	Sea Nocturne/*Glenda Austin*	$2.99
00416844 ____	Sea Tempest/*Randall Hartsell*	$2.99
00415517 ____	Sonatine/*William Gillock*	$2.99
00416701 ____	Spanish Romance/*arr. Frank Levin*	$2.95
00416946 ____	Stormy Seas/*Carolyn Miller*	$2.99
00416100 ____	Three Jazz Preludes/*William Gillock*	$3.95

Later Intermediate

00416715 ____	Hear the Spirit of America/*Marilyn Briant and Andrew Zatman*	$2.95
00416764 ____	Romantic Rhapsody/*Glenda Austin*	$2.95
00405646 ____	Soft Lights/*Carolyn Jones Campbell*	$1.95
00409464 ____	Tarantella/*A. Pieczonka*	$2.95

Early Advanced

00415263 ____	Impromptu/*Mildred T. Souers*	$2.95
00415166 ____	Sleighbells in the Snow/*William Gillock*	$2.95
00405264 ____	Valse Brillante/*Glenda Austin*	$2.95

HAL•LEONARD® CORPORATION

7777 W. BLUEMOUND RD. P.O. BOX 13819 MILWAUKEE, WI 53213

CLOSER LOOK View sample pages and hear audio excerpts online at **www.halleonard.com**

  www.facebook.com/willispianomusic

Prices & availability subject to change without notice.

0412

A DOZEN A DAY

by Edna Mae Burnam

The **A Dozen A Day** books are universally recognized as one of the most remarkable technique series on the market for all ages! Each book in this series contains short warm-up exercises to be played at the beginning of each practice session, providing excellent day-to-day training for the student. The CD is playable on any CD player and features fabulous backing tracks by Ric Iannone. For Windows® and Mac users, the CD is enhanced so you can access MIDI files for each exercise and adjust the tempo.

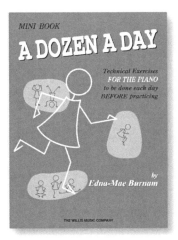
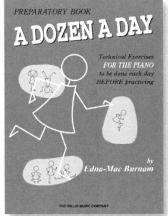
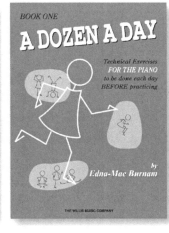
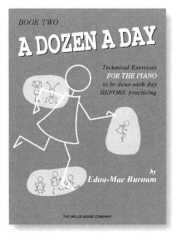

MINI BOOK
00404073 Book Only $3.99
00406472 Book/CD $8.99

PREPARATORY BOOK
00414222 Book Only $3.99
00406476 Book/CD $8.99

BOOK 1
00413366 Book Only $3.99
00406481 Book/CD $8.99

BOOK 2
00413826 Book Only $3.99
00406485 Book/CD $8.99

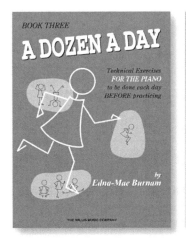

BOOK 3
00414136 Book Only $4.99
00416760 Book/CD $9.99

BOOK 4
00415686 Book Only $5.99
00416761 Book/CD $10.99

**PLAY WITH EASE
IN MANY KEYS**
00416395 Book Only $3.95

WILLIS MUSIC

EXCLUSIVELY DISTRIBUTED BY

HAL•LEONARD®

CLASSIC PIANO
REPERTOIRE